DATE DUE

Pebble® Plus
Bilingüe/ Bilingual

Comida sana con MiPirámide/Healthy Eating with MyPyramid

Meriendas saludables/Healthy Snacks

por/by Mari C. Schuh

Traducción/Translation: Dr. Martín Luis Guzmán Ferrer
Editor Consultor/Consulting Editor: Dra. Gail Saunders-Smith

Consultor/Consultant: Barbara J. Rolls, PhD
Guthrie Chair in Nutrition
The Pennsylvania State University
University Park, Pennsylvania

Capstone
press®
Mankato, Minnesota

Pebble Plus is published by Capstone Press,
151 Good Counsel Drive, P.O. Box 669, Mankato, Minnesota 56002.
www.capstonepress.com

1 2 3 4 5 6 11 10 09 08 07 06

Library of Congress Cataloging-in-Publication Data
Schuh, Mari C., 1975–
    [Healthy snacks. English & Spanish]
    Meriendas saludables/de Mari C. Schuh = Healthy snacks/by Mari C. Schuh.
    p. cm.—(Comida sana con MiPirámide = Healthy eating with MyPyramid)
    title: Healthy snacks.
    Includes index.
    Parallel text in English and Spanish.
    ISBN-13: 978-0-7368-6671-2 (hardcover)
    ISBN-10: 0-7368-6671-X (hardcover)
    1. Snack foods—Juvenile literature. 2. Nutrition—Juvenile literature. I. Title: Healthy snacks. II. Title.
TX740.S325718 2007
641.5'39—dc22   2005037341

Summary: Simple text and photographs present healthy snacks, examples of healthy snacks, and ways to enjoy
    healthy snacks—in both English and Spanish.

Credits
 Katy Kudela, bilingual editor; Eida del Risco, Spanish copy editor; Jennifer Bergstrom, designer;
    Kelly Garvin, photo researcher; Stacy Foster, photo shoot coordinator

Photo Credits
Capstone Press/Karon Dubke, all except U.S. Department of Agriculture, 8 (inset), 9 (computer screen)

Capstone Press thanks Hilltop Hy-Vee employees in Mankato, Minnesota, for their helpful assistance with
photo shoots.

**Information in this book supports the U.S. Department of Agriculture's MyPyramid for Kids
food guidance system found at http://www.MyPyramid.gov/kids.**

**The U.S. Department of Agriculture (USDA) does not endorse any products, services,
or organizations.**

Note to Parents and Teachers

The Comida sana con MiPirámide/Healthy Eating with MyPyramid set supports national science standards related to nutrition and physical health. This book describes healthy snacks in both English and Spanish. The images support early readers in understanding the text. The repetition of words and phrases helps early readers learn new words. This book also introduces early readers to subject-specific vocabulary words, which are defined in the Glossary section. Early readers may need assistance to read some words and to use the Table of Contents, Glossary, Internet Sites, and Index sections of the book.

Table of Contents

Tabla de contenidos

Healthy Snacks

Snacks are foods you eat when you
are hungry between meals.
Small healthy snacks
help you grow strong.

Meriendas saludables

Las meriendas son alimentos que
tomas entre las comidas cuando
tienes hambre. Las meriendas
sanas te ayudan a crecer fuerte.

A healthy snack gives you
energy until your next meal.
What snacks have you
eaten today?

Una merienda saludable te da
energía hasta tu próxima comida.
¿Qué has merendado hoy?

MyPyramid for Kids

Learn more about healthy snacks and healthy eating from MyPyramid. MyPyramid is a tool to help you eat healthy food.

MiPirámide para niños

En MiPirámide puedes conocer más sobre meriendas y comidas saludables. MiPirámide es una herramienta para ayudarte a comer alimentos sanos.

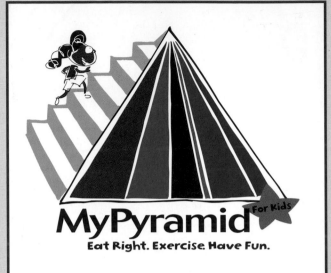

MyPyramid For Kids
Eat Right. Exercise. Have Fun.

To learn more about
healthy eating,
go to this web site:
www.MyPyramid.gov/kids
Ask an adult for help.

Para saber más sobre
comida sana ve a este
sitio de Internet:
www.MyPyramid.gov/kids
Pídele a un adulto
que te ayude.

MyPyramid shows you
all the food groups.
You can choose healthy snacks
from every food group.

MiPirámide muestra todos
los grupos de alimentos.
Puedes escoger meriendas
saludables de cada uno
de estos grupos.

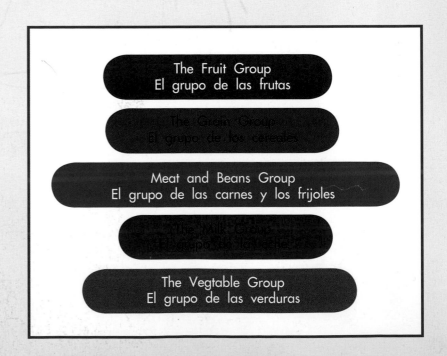

The Fruit Group
El grupo de las frutas

The Grain Group
El grupo de los cereales

Meat and Beans Group
El grupo de las carnes y los frijoles

The Milk Group
El grupo de la leche

The Vegtable Group
El grupo de las verduras

11

Enjoying Healthy Snacks

Got the munchies?

A small bowl

of low-fat popcorn makes

a great afternoon snack.

Cómo disfrutar las meriendas saludables

¿Quieres algo de merienda?

Un plato pequeño de palomitas

bajas en grasas constituye

una merienda deliciosa.

Mmmm! Carrots and celery taste yummy dipped in salad dressing. What's your favorite vegetable snack?

¡Mmmm! Las zanahorias o el apio saben riquísimos con un aderezo para ensaladas. ¿Cuál es la verdura que más te gusta de merienda?

Are you thirsty?
Make a smoothie
with your favorite yogurt
and fruit. Gulp!

¿Tienes sed? Haz un
licuado con tu fruta y
tu yogurt favoritos. ¡Glup!

Nibble, nibble, nibble.
Whole-wheat crackers
topped with cheese
can fill you up.

Picar, picar, picar.
Las galletas de trigo integral
con una lasquita de queso
te dejan más que satisfecho.

It's easy and fun
to make healthy snacks.
Healthy food fuels your body.
Enjoy!

Es muy fácil y divertido
preparar meriendas saludables.
La comida saludable le da energía
a tu cuerpo. ¡Que te aproveche!

Healthy Snack Ideas/Ideas para meriendas saludables

If you have the munchies between meals, eat a small healthy snack. Small snacks will fuel your body until your next meal.

Si tienes ganas de comer algo entre comidas, come un merienda pequeña y sana. Los meriendas pequeñas le dan energía a tu cuerpo hasta la siguiente comida.

Try one of these foods the next time you get hungry between meals!

¡Prueba alguno de estos alimentos la próxima vez que tengas hambre entre las comidas!

vegetable soup
sopa de verduras

fresh fruit
fruta fresca

string cheese
tiritas de queso

carrots and low-fat dip
zanahorias con aderezo
bajo en grasas

sliced orange
rebanadas de naranja

cherry tomatoes
tomatitos

cereal with fruit
cereal con fruta

sunflower seeds
semillas de girasol

Glossary

energy—the strength to be active without getting tired

MyPyramid—a food plan that helps kids make healthy food choices and reminds kids to be active; MyPyramid was created by the U.S. Department of Agriculture.

smoothie—a thick, smooth drink made by mixing ice, milk or juice, low-fat yogurt, and fruit in a blender

Glosario

la energía—fuerza que te permite estar activo sin cansarte

el licuado—bebida espesa y suave hecha con hielo, leche o jugo, yogurt bajo en grasas y frutas en una licuadora

MiPirámide—plan de alimentos que ayuda a los chicos a escoger comidas saludables y a mantenerse activos; MiPirámide fue creada por el Departamento de Agricultura de los Estados Unidos.

Index

Índice

Internet Sites

FactHound offers a safe, fun way to find Internet sites related to this book. All of the sites on FactHound have been researched by our staff.

Here's how:

1. Visit *www.facthound.com*

2. Choose your grade level.

3. Type in this book ID **073686671X** for age-appropriate sites. You may also browse subjects by clicking on letters, or by clicking on pictures and words.

4. Click on the **Fetch It** button.

FactHound will fetch the best sites for you!

Sitios de Internet

FactHound proporciona una manera divertida y segura de encontrar sitios de Internet relacionados con este libro. Nuestro personal ha investigado todos los sitios de FactHound. Es posible que los sitios no estén en español.

Se hace así:

1. Visita *www.facthound.com*

2. Elige tu grado escolar.

3. Introduce este código especial **073686671X** para ver sitios apropiados según tu edad, o usa una palabra relacionada con este libro para hacer una búsqueda general.

4. Haz clic en el botón **Fetch It**.

¡FactHound buscará los mejores sitios para ti!